# TUNDRA

## APRIL PULLEY SAYRE

**TWENTY-FIRST CENTURY BOOKS**

A Division of Henry Holt and Company
• New York •

*For my mother, Elizabeth Richardson Pulley, who leads me to adventure.*
*~ A.P.S. ~*

---

## ACKNOWLEDGMENTS

Thanks to the scientists who reviewed or helped with the research for this manuscript: biologist Pam Miller, Assistant Regional Director of the Wilderness Society in Alaska; and Mike Emers and Janet Jorgenson, botanists at the Arctic National Wildlife Refuge, also in Alaska.

---

Twenty-First Century Books
A Division of Henry Holt and Company, Inc.
115 West 18th Street
New York, NY 10011

Henry Holt ® and colophon are trademarks of
Henry Holt and Company, Inc.
*Publishers since 1866*

Published in Canada by Fitzhenry & Whiteside Ltd.
195 Allstate Parkway, Markham, Ontario L3R 4T8

**Library of Congress Cataloging-in-Publication Data**
Sayre, April Pulley.
Tundra / April Pulley Sayre. —1st ed.
p. cm. — (Exploring earth's biomes)
Includes index.
1. Tundra ecology—Juvenile literature. 2. Tundras—Juvenile literature. 3. Tundra ecology—Arctic regions—Juvenile literature. 4. Tundras—Arctic regions—Juvenile literature. [1. Tundras. 2. Arctic regions. 3. Tundra ecology. 4. Ecology.] I. Title. II. Series: Sayre, April Pulley. Exploring earth's biomes.
QH541.5.T8S28 1994                          574.5'2644—dc20
                                                              94–19385

ISBN 0-8050-2829-3
First Edition 1994

**Photo Credits**
p. 8: Tom Bean; p. 20: Johnny Johnson/Alaska Stock Images; pp. 21, 38: Dan Guravich/Photo Researchers, Inc.; p. 30: Breck P. Kent/Earth Scenes; p. 32: George Calef/Masterfile; p. 35: Wayne Lynch/Masterfile; p. 43: Tom McHugh/Photo Researchers, Inc.; p. 51: Chris Arend/Alaska Stock Images.

# CONTENTS

❦

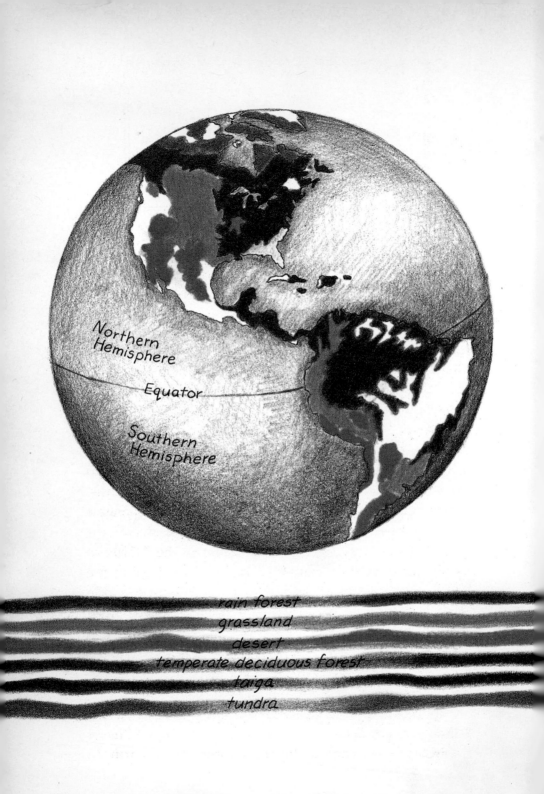

Northern
Hemisphere

Equator

Southern
Hemisphere

rain forest
grassland
desert
temperate deciduous forest
taiga
tundra

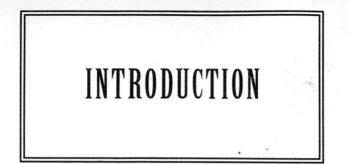

# INTRODUCTION

Take a look at the earth as a whole and you'll see its surface can be divided into living communities called biomes. Desert, rain forest, tundra, taiga, temperate deciduous forest, grassland, and polar desert are some of the main terrestrial biomes—biomes on land. Each biome has particular kinds of plants and animals living in it. Scientists also identify other biomes not mentioned here, including aquatic biomes—biomes of lakes, streams, and the sea.

When their boundaries are drawn on a globe, terrestrial biomes look like horizontal bands stacked up from Pole to Pole. Starting from the equator and moving outward toward the Poles, you'll find rain forests, grasslands, deserts, and grasslands once again. Then things change a little. The next biomes we think of—temperate deciduous forests, taiga, and tundra—exist only in the Northern Hemisphere. Why is this true? Well, if you look in the Southern Hemisphere, you'll see there's very little land in the regions where these biomes would supposedly lie. There's simply nowhere for these biomes to exist! Conditions on small pieces of land—islands and peninsulas—that lie in these areas are greatly affected by sea conditions and are very different from those on continents.

But why do biomes generally develop in these bands? The answer lies in the earth's climate and geology. Climate is affected by the angle at which sunlight hits the earth. At the equator, sunlight passes through the atmosphere and hits the earth straight on, giving it its full energy. At the Poles, sunlight must pass through more atmosphere and it hits the earth at an angle, with less energy per square foot. Other factors also influence where biomes lie: the bands of rising and falling air that circulate around the planet; the complex weather systems created by jutting mountains, deep valleys, and cold currents; the glaciers that have scoured the lands in years past; and the activities of humans. These make biome boundaries less regular than the simplified bands described above.

# *1*
# THE TUNDRA BIOME

At ten o'clock in the morning, the sky is dark and you haven't seen the sun for almost 40 days. It's wintertime in Alaska, on the treeless land called tundra. The temperature is -22°F (-30°C), but the windchill makes it feel much colder. To stay warm, musk oxen huddle in their long shaggy coats. Lemmings burrow beneath a crust of snow. And arctic foxes, their white coats barely visible against the snow, stalk ptarmigans, lemmings, or whatever else they can find.

On a winter day like this, it's hard to imagine that summer ever comes to the tundra. Yet in late May, when the days become long and the sun only briefly disappears below the horizon, the snow *will* melt. The top layer of ground will thaw. Plants will turn green, and flowers—millions of tiny flowers—will carpet the tundra with color.

Migrating caribou will return from the south to graze on these plants. Sandpipers will search ponds and streams for insects, while arctic terns hover then swoop to grab fish. Grizzly bears, black bears, and people will fill up on the summer feast of berries, while billions of mosquitoes fill up on the blood of bears, people, and caribou.

The Arctic tundra is a biome—a geographic area that has a particular type of animal and plant community living within it. The word *tundra,* in the Russian language, means a treeless, marshy area. That's a good description of these lands, which are dotted with ponds and support only low-

*South of the Arctic you can hike through alpine tundra, an ecological community similar but not identical to Arctic tundra, which occurs farther north.*

growing plants. Three million square miles (7,800,000 square kilometers) of Arctic tundra stretch across the northern portions of Alaska, Canada, Greenland, Iceland, Russia, and the Scandinavian countries: Norway, Finland, Denmark, and Sweden.

Yet much farther south, in isolated patches on mountainsides in the Colorado Rockies, the Cascades, and other mountain ranges, you can also find another type of tundra called alpine tundra. Alpine tundra has cold and windy weather, and has low-growing plants like the Arctic tundra. But alpine regions get more rain, have soil that drains better, and receive more sunlight than Arctic tundra. The two biomes have some different plants and animals, too.

This book will deal primarily with Arctic tundra. Stretching in a band near the top of the earth, it's a place where quick freezes and slow thaws create strange bumps, cracks, and patterns in the land. It's a place where bright streaks of blue, pink, and white can paint the winter nighttime sky. And despite its cold climate, many fascinating creatures thrive in this harsh environment.

### TYPES

There are two main types of tundra: Arctic tundra and alpine tundra.

- Arctic tundra occurs close to sea level in the Arctic.
- Alpine tundra occurs in isolated patches on mountainsides from the Arctic to as far south as Central America.

### TEMPERATURES

- Air temperature varies widely during the year, with generally warm summers and cold winters.
- Average yearly temperature range: -70°F to 20°F (-57°C to -7°C ) in winter and 30°F to 60°F (-1°C to 16°C ) in summer.

### WEATHER

- Tundra gets a considerable amount of snow in winter and a little bit of rain in summer. But total precipitation is just 4 to 20 inches (10 to 50 centimeters) per year, with some places getting only as much precipitation as desert.
- Wind drifts snow to great depths around riverbanks and buildings, but overall, snow depth tends to be less than you might expect in such a cold land.
- Despite the low precipitation, average humidity is high, because there is little warmth to evaporate the water that is present.
- Summers are often cloudy. Weather may be erratic, with sudden snowstorms in the midst of hot summer.
- Winds can be strong, from 30 to 60 miles per hour (48 to 97 kilometers per hour).

### SOIL

- The most distinctive characteristic of tundra soil is its permafrost, a permanently frozen layer of ground 1,300 to 2,000 feet (400 to 600 meters) thick.

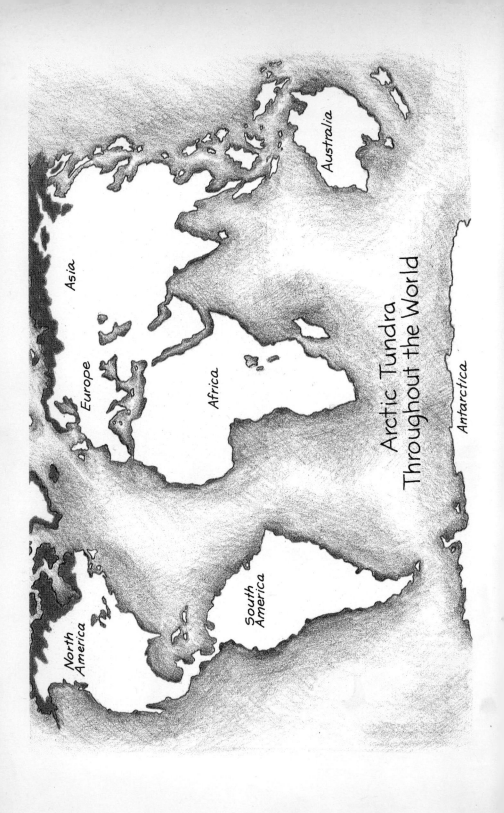

Arctic Tundra Throughout the World

- Above the permafrost is an active layer of soil that thaws in the summer although it refreezes in winter.
- Plants grow roots and microorganisms live in this active layer, which averages 20 inches (50 centimeters) deep.
- Tundra soils vary, but are typically low in the minerals and organic matter needed for plant growth.

## PLANTS

- Shallow-rooted and low growing, tundra plants often form lumpy mats. Most plants are perennials, with underground roots that survive year after year.
- Aboveground, the tundra's plant biomass—the total weight of plant matter for a given area—is generally lower than in other biomes, except for some deserts. In many tundra areas there is as much or more plant biomass belowground as above.
- Common plants: mosses, sedges, small shrubs, buttercups, poppies, willows, and saxifrage.
- Also common are lichens—a living partnership between fungi and algae. Living among mosses in dry areas, and coating rocks and bare ground, lichen grows in crusty-looking forms of black, orange, gray, white, or yellow.

## ANIMALS

- Arctic tundra has a lower species diversity—fewer animal and plant species—than most other biomes, except the driest desert. But tundra may have large numbers of those species that do occur.
- Animals are adapted to handle cold winters and to breed and raise young quickly in the short Arctic summer.
- Animal populations may fluctuate widely, rising in number over several years, then sharply dropping in size.
- Many animals have a circumpolar distribution, meaning they occur in Arctic regions on various continents and islands around the North Pole.

# *❧*2*❧*
# TUNDRA IN
# NORTH AMERICA

Walking north through the pine and spruce forests of Canada, eventually you'll reach a place where the trees just run out. Beyond is the North American tundra, a land of low-growing shrubs, mosses, lichens, and grasses. Stretching in a band along the northern edges of Canada and Alaska, over portions of Greenland and other islands in the Arctic Ocean, this biome is wild and vast.

The tundra itself is a complex patchwork of many different plant communities—groups of plant species that grow together. Water-loving plants grow beside tundra ponds, while on better-drained hilltops, plants that cope well with dryness and wind hug the ground. In well-drained sand or gravel soils near Arctic rivers, tall shrubs such as willow, birch, and alder grow. In the southern tundra, valleys or stream banks may shelter stunted trees.

Almost 20 percent of the earth's land surface is tundra. Looking out over the North American tundra, you'll see a sight similar to what a person in Asia might see on the Siberian tundra. That is because many tundra animals and plants have a circumpolar distribution, meaning they occur all the way around one of the earth's poles, in this case, the North Pole. In the Arctic, where the northern rims of several continents exist close together, animal and plant species can easily spread from one continent to another.

Thousands of years ago, land animals could walk

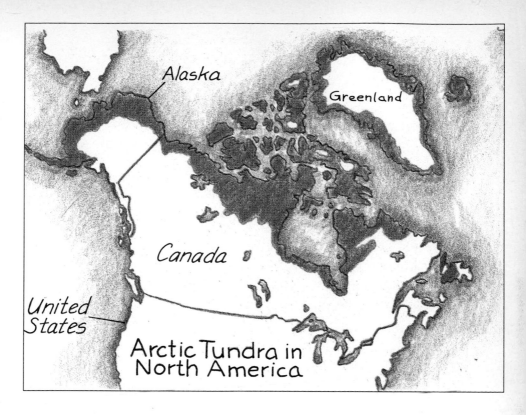

Arctic Tundra in
North America

directly from North America to Asia on a land bridge now covered by the waters of the Bering Strait. Even today animals need only swim across short distances to reach islands and other continents. In winter, foxes, caribou, and musk oxen walk across frozen-over ocean to reach Arctic islands. By air, birds can fly a relatively short distance—2 ½ miles (4 kilometers)—to get from the United States to the former Soviet Republic. Plant seeds can make such journeys, too, when they are spread by wind, or carried on animals' fur or feathers. This global exchange of animals and plants is only one of the many features that makes the Arctic tundra so fascinating. Below are some other remarkable facts about North America's tundra:

• Greenland, the largest island in the world, is considered by geographers to be part of the North American continent. It's often described as an ice-filled bowl, with mountain ranges making up the edges of the bowl. On the bowl's outer edges, the seaward side, is a small fringe of tundra. Five-sixths of this island is covered by ice.

- Little Diomede Island is part of the United States, while Big Diomede Island is part of what was once the Union of Soviet Socialist Republics. Because the international date line runs between the two islands, when it is Sunday in Little Diomede, it is Monday in Big Diomede, only 2 ½ miles (4 kilometers) away.

- In 1867, the United States purchased Alaska from Russia for $7.2 million, about 2 cents per acre. The purchase, which was negotiated by Secretary of State William H. Seward, was often called "Seward's Folly," because people at the time thought Alaska was useless land.

- The coastal plain of the Arctic National Wildlife Refuge in Alaska is the calving grounds of a 180,000-member caribou herd, and habitat for polar bears, grizzlies, wolves, musk oxen, and birds. Oil companies want to drill here and environmentalists oppose such drilling.

- Bering Land Bridge National Preserve protects Alaska's section of a land bridge that connected North America and Asia 13,000 years ago. The nesting site of millions of migratory birds, this preserve and the portion of the land bridge in Russia, 55 miles (89 kilometers) away, are part of a proposed International Peace Park.

- Baffin Island, located in northeastern Canada, contains sections of tundra and is the homeland of many Inuit— Native Americans sometimes referred to as Eskimo. Polar bears, arctic foxes, and caribou inhabit the tundra and walruses, seals, whales, and narwhals inhabit the surrounding ocean.

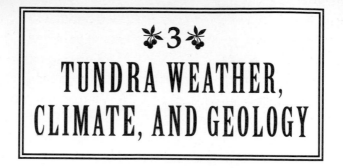

# ❈ 3 ❈
# TUNDRA WEATHER, CLIMATE, AND GEOLOGY

With strangely painted skies and sunlight that lasts for days, the tundra can come as something of a shock to visitors from other biomes. Where else can you trek across a landscape that looks like it has been sculpted by playful giants—with striped hillsides, doughnut-shaped pebble piles, and water-filled trenches that honeycomb the soil? Where else can you stand on frozen ground so deep and ancient, it holds the carcasses of mammoths that lived 30,000 years before you were born? Nowhere else; no other biome has the same extreme climate or the mystery and marvel of the tundra landscape.

## LANDS OF THE MIDNIGHT SUN

Up near the top of the world, where the tundra lies, are the lands of the midnight sun. In the summer, days here are long—very long. For 84 days, from late May to early August, the sun doesn't set on the tundra near Barrow, Alaska. The sun shines even at midnight, although it is very low in the sky. But time here isn't all sun-filled. Arctic tundra residents "pay" for these sunny summers. They endure 66 days, from mid-November to late January, when it's totally dark, and the sun doesn't peek above the horizon at all.

**It's the Tilt**    The reason the Arctic tundra has this drastic day and night cycle is the tilt of the earth's axis and the position of the Arctic tundra near the North Pole.

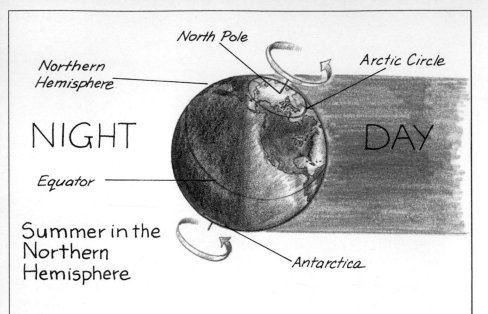

North Pole

Arctic Circle

Northern
Hemisphere

NIGHT

DAY

Equator

Summer in the
Northern
Hemisphere

Antarctica

*The earth spins on its axis, creating a cycle of day and night. During
June and July, Arctic tundra lands, because of their location near the
North Pole, do not move out of reach of the sun's rays.*

Because of the earth's position relative to the sun, in June
and July regions near the North Pole experience 24 hours of
daylight per day. As the earth spins on its daily cycle, these
regions never move out of reach of the sun's rays. The oppo-
site is true in December and January, when these northern
regions experience 24 hours of darkness per day, because
the sun's rays then cannot reach that part of the earth. In
Antarctica, the seasons are reversed. Long days of summer
are in December and January, while long nights of winter
are in June and July.

Conditions are much different at the equator. Every
day of the year, these regions move into the path of the sun's
rays during the day, and revolve out of reach of the sun's
rays at night. Days and nights are almost the same length all
year long.

## WHERE YOU'LL FIND ARCTIC TUNDRA

Arctic tundra is located in the Arctic, a region that looks like a cap on the earth, with the North Pole at its center. The confusing thing about the Arctic is that not all scientists agree on its boundaries. Most globes have a line at 66° latitude called the Arctic Circle. But this is not what most biologists consider the boundary of the Arctic.

Biologists define the Arctic as an area around the North Pole where the average temperature of the warmest month is not more than 50°F (10°C). Because this boundary depends on temperature, it's called an isotherm. This isotherm is north of the Arctic Circle.

**A Band Around the Earth**   South of the tundra band is the taiga, a biome nicknamed "spruce-moose" because it has spruce trees, a mossy forest floor, and often, moose. North of the tundra is the polar desert, pebbled ground with only small patches of plants. Farther north, where even these small patches of plants can't grow, is an icy region where polar bears hunt seals along the Arctic Ocean. This ice rests not on land, but on ocean, where it floats, with some of the ice above, and some below, the water. It creates an icy bridge that connects small islands that exist in the Arctic region, allowing foxes, bears, and people, too, to cross over ice to reach other islands in winter.

## TUNDRA WEATHER AND TUNDRA SOILS

Over the course of a year, temperatures can vary widely in the tundra. Winter temperatures can drop to a bone-chilling -70°F (-57°C). And the windchill factor from high winds can make that temperature feel much colder. Yet the strange thing is that in summer, Arctic tundra areas can experience quite warm days, with temperatures in the 60s°F (16°C to 20°C). Occasionally they even soar into the low 80s°F (27°C to 28°C)!

**Frozen Ground** Permafrost, or frozen ground, is an important feature of the tundra environment. It influences geology and limits plant growth in the region. In some places, this frozen ground is 2,000 feet (600 meters) deep! During the winter, all the soil is frozen. But during the spring, when days lengthen and temperatures rise, the top soil layer thaws. This is the active layer, where biological action takes place. Here plant roots grow, animals burrow, and soil microorganisms decompose dead animals and plants. The shallowness of the active layer is one factor that prevents trees from growing in the tundra. Trees need to establish deep roots to grow but cannot because of permanently frozen ground. Temperature and lack of nutrients also limit their growth.

---

### • THAT SINKING FEELING •

If you built your house directly on tundra, it would likely sink. The heat from the house would warm the ground and cause the permafrost to melt, so the land underneath would become soggy and unstable. To solve this problem, some people build their houses on stilts—long pilings driven deep into the earth. This creates a space under the house so the heated homes won't melt the permafrost. Others build houses on layers of coarse gravel, which also help prevent the heat from reaching the permafrost.

---

**Mysterious Mammoths** In the tundra's super refrigerator, the permafrost, entire animals—not just bones, but hair and skin, too—can be preserved for hundreds and thousands of years. In 1951, scientists in Alaska dug up the well-preserved carcass of an animal called "superbison" that was more than 31,000 years old! In the former Soviet Union, people have found almost 120,000 woolly mammoth carcasses.

**Nutrient-poor Soils**   Even the active layer of soil is generally deficient in nutrients good for plant growth. Because of the cold, rock weathering and decomposition of dead plants and animals—two major sources of soil nutrients—take place at very slow rates. So the soil remains nutrient poor.

**The Strange Case of the Soggy Soil**   The tundra receives only about 12 to 20 inches (31 to 51 centimeters) of snow in a year. If you melt that down and add it to the rain the tundra gets, the yearly average precipitation is low, not much more than a desert receives. Yet most Arctic tundra is wet. This is because the permafrost layer, which lies below the ground surface, prevents what water does arrive from seeping away. And very little of the water evaporates because the air is cool and the sunlight the tundra receives is not very strong. (The sun hits polar areas such as the tundra at an angle. Solar energy is not as direct and concentrated as it is at the equator.) Snow and ice also reflect much of the sunlight back into the air.

## MYSTERIOUS COLORS IN THE SKY: THE NORTHERN LIGHTS

Sometimes, most often during the long nights of winter, there's a light show in Arctic skies. Great blazes of rose, white, and green appear, like bright paints brushed across the sky. These colors may last for many minutes and return several times in a single night. This is the aurora borealis—the northern lights. People who live near the South Pole see a similar light show, called the aurora australis, or the southern lights. The lights near both the North and South Poles are caused by the sun, which occasionally sends out highly charged particles that interact with the earth's magnetic field.

*The aurora borealis, a dazzling display of colored lights, occasionally appears in Arctic skies in winter.*

## FROZEN FORMS

Flying over the Arctic tundra you can see strange, almost mysterious shapes, forms, and patterns. This land is sculpted by the power of water—not rushing water, for the most part, but freezing water. The soils have been molded by the freezing and thawing of water, year after year after year. Just look at some of the odd shapes these forces create in the tundra:

- **Pingos**  These conical hills are formed when water collects in a small pool underground and is trapped there by permafrost. Yearly freezing and thawing makes a pingo grow taller, inches at a time. It may get to be as tall as 150 feet (46 meters).
- **Polygons**  These irregular, many-sided geometric land shapes are 10 to 100 feet (3 to 30 meters) wide and are outlined by water-filled cracks. The cracks often broaden,

forming streams and sometimes shallow ponds, connected like beads on a string. The polygons can have high ridges between them, or have high centers.

- **Bumpy and Lumpy Ground** Rocks, small ponds, and mounds of plants affect the rates at which soils freeze and thaw. As a result, sections of ground may expand and contract, as they freeze and thaw, pushing against one another, forming bumps, hills, and tiny valleys.
- **Stone Circles** When water freezes and expands, it pushes out on the rocks around it. Over time, continual freezing and thawing can thrust large rocks outward, in ever-widening circles called frost boils. Eventually, only tiny rock or sand grains remain in the center, while large rocks form a surrounding circle, a doughnut-shaped pebble pile.

*These twin pingos are the result of land sculpted by the power of freezing water.*

- **Stripes**   On hillsides, freezing and thawing sort small rocks and dirt according to particle size, creating a soil pattern of visible stripes.

**Rivers of Ice**   Giant rivers of ice, called glaciers, also shape Arctic lands. Glaciers are formed when snow does not melt and so builds up year after year. The weight of the built-up snow presses down on snow below it, creating an ultra-dense ice called firn. Eventually, a glacier's weight makes the ice move, flowing slowly along the land or into the sea.

During the ice ages much of the earth was covered with ice. But when the world warmed, glaciers melted and retreated, leaving behind rocks and other materials they once carried. Today's glaciers are only remnants, draped over mountain ranges, hanging poised above the sea. But there are lots of glacier-created landforms the world over. In the tundra, long ridges of gravel, called eskers, mark where glaciers dropped their loads. And long scratches on rocks indicate where a glacier full of silt scraped across the land, like slowly moving sandpaper.

**Land of Change**   Freezing and thawing are not the only forces that shape the tundra. Volcanoes thrust up mountains, and earthquakes shake the land, causing landslides and other geologic shifts. The force of gravity, too, is at work. In the tundra, the force of gravity causes soggy soil to flow downhill by a process called solifluction. (The soil is soggy because water cannot run off into the frozen permafrost underneath.) These slow-motion landslides can bury plants. They are just one of the remarkable features of this ever-changing land.

# *❋4❋*
# TUNDRA PLANTS

The Arctic tundra is not a plant-growing paradise. The sun—the source of plants' energy—barely peeks above the horizon for half the year. The shallow, nutrient-poor soil is only free of snow for two to three months per year. And plants have to contend with cold temperatures that can freeze and rupture their tissues.

Yet despite these conditions, some plants do thrive in the tundra. In summer, hills and valleys blaze with red, yellow, orange, and blue flowers. For a few brief, glorious months, long, sunny days give plants the burst of energy they need to grow, flower, and produce new tissues that will carry them through the next Arctic winter.

## THE TUNDRA YEAR

Through the dark, cold months of winter, most plants are covered with snow. Snow acts as a blanket, protecting plants from cold, chilling winds, and low air temperatures. Only the very tips of some alder and willow shrubs peek out above the surface of the snow.

**Coming to Life**  In May, when the days grow longer, some sunlight penetrates the snow. A few plants can make use of this light and begin photosynthesis while still snow-covered. But most growth does not occur until the snow has melted or perhaps even later, when the top few inches of ground have thawed. Melting can occur irregularly; some patches melt right away, while snowdrifts remain in low-lying areas well into July. And each year, the timing and duration of the snowmelt varies.

**All in a Rush**   Tundra plants grow, flower, and set seed quickly. They have to, in order to pack all their activity into the short Arctic growing season. This season lasts only 10 to 14 weeks, from June through August. During that time the sun shines practically all day long. Although the sunlight shining on the polar regions is energetically weak, at this time of year the tundra may actually receive as much solar energy in a day as the tropics do. That's because the sun shines on the tundra for so long—as much as 24 hours per day, while it shines at the equator for only about 12 hours per day.

**Dormant Again**   In the fall, plant fluids and pigments drain out of leaves and shoots and are stored in roots or bulbs. The leftover pigments in the leaves give tundra plants bright orange, yellow, and red colors. These fall colors are a low-growing version of the fall display put on by temperate deciduous forest trees. This color change indicates plants are shutting down for the dark, cold winter ahead.

## STRATEGIES FOR SURVIVAL

Over thousands of years, tundra plants have evolved to grow well in the cold, uncertain weather conditions in this biome. Even during the brief growing season, plants may encounter cold, frost, or snow. Early spring blizzards after the snowmelt are not uncommon; they may occur even in July. Below are some of the adaptations that help plants survive in this environment.

**Cool by Nature**   Arctic tundra plants are adapted to carry on photosynthesis and to grow at cool temperatures. Their shoots grow best at temperatures 27°F to 36°F (15°C to 20°C) cooler than plants in the temperate zone.

**Small and Low-growing**   One thing you immediately notice about tundra plants is that most are small and low-growing. Lack of nutrients may limit plant growth and height. But another reason for this low growth is that the air is warmer near the ground. The ground is dark-colored and easily absorbs heat, so the air near it is warmer. For taller tundra plants such as willows, winter snow depth usually limits height. Stems sticking up above the snow can be ground away by ice and snow blowing along the surface. So tundra shrubs generally grow only about as tall as the snow is deep, with the tallest growing in gullies where snowdrifts form.

**Hairy and Dark**   To warm up quickly and stay warm in cold conditions, many tundra plants are dark-colored and hairy. Dark surfaces warm up more quickly than lighter-colored surfaces. Hair traps this warmth against the plant's surface, insulating it from the cold. Willow, a common tundra plant, forms fuzzy, insulating coverings on its buds, called catkins. Soft as a kitten's tail, these structures are related to the fuzzy pussy willows seen in gardens around the world.

**Cushions, Clumps, and Tussocks**   Walking across the tundra can be slow going, because clumps of cotton grass create tiny hills, an uneven, spongy surface that can easily turn an ankle. By growing in clumps, these plants stay warmer. Overlapping leaves create a tiny, warm environment that is protected from the wind. The rounded hills, made entirely of plants, are called tussocks. Their shape helps to break the wind and expose more of the plant to the sun, warming it further.

**Staying Green**  When winter arrives, many plants drop their leaves and die back to just a root. But some plants keep their leaves in order to get a "head start" on the next year's growing season. Plants that keep their leaves over one winter then drop them late in the next growing season are called wintergreens. Plants that keep leaves longer are called evergreens.

**Shallow Roots**  Tundra plants are shallow-rooted because they cannot grow downward into the permafrost, which lies anywhere from several inches to a few feet below the ground's surface. Even if plant roots did enter the permafrost, they wouldn't get much in the way of nutrients. Much more nutrient matter is available for plants in the active layer—the shallow, thawed region above the permafrost. Microorganisms live in this active layer; plant and animal matter decays. And snowmelt penetrates, carrying nutrients into the soil.

# SOLAR WARMING

Why are tundra plants often dark in color? The answer is related to how they absorb the sun's warmth. Try this experiment to see which surfaces absorb more warmth: dark ones or light ones.

You'll need:
- Thin black plastic (a black garbage bag works well)
- Thin white plastic (a shopping bag or white garbage bag works well)
- Four aluminum pie pans or four other same-size shallow pans
- Eight or more cups (two liters) of water, of constant temperature
- A thermometer

- Masking tape
- Scissors
- Pencil and paper
- Watch or clock
- An area in the sun and an area in the shade where your experiment will be undisturbed

**1.** Measure and cut a piece of the white plastic bag to line one of the pie pans. Then cut another white piece of plastic and two black pieces of plastic the same size as the first.

**2.** Line the pie pans with the plastic pieces. Use tape, where needed, to fasten the plastic to the plate and keep it from pouching out.

**3.** Place a white-lined pan and a black-lined pan in the shade, and a white-lined pan and a black-lined pan in the sun. Be sure they are resting on the same kinds of surfaces. (If one were on black asphalt and another on grass, that would change your results.)

**4.** Pour two cups (one-half liter) of water into each pie pan. They should be a little over half full.

**5.** Test the temperature of the water in each pan right away. They should all be the same.

**6.** Leave the pans, returning every 15 minutes to measure the temperature of the water in each pan. Do this for two hours. Record your results.

Which sets of pans showed a difference in temperature between them at the end of the period? Which were the same? What do your results show about the relationship between color and heat absorption? To maximize heat absorption, what color should a tundra plant be?

## LIFE CYCLES: THE NEXT GENERATION

Most tundra plants are perennials—plants that don't die in winter, but instead survive with their leaves, shoots, or perhaps just roots in the ground. Perennials start out the next season with already established growth and flower much sooner. This gives them a big advantage over annuals— plants that grow from seed to seed-bearing plant in one growing season, then die off. With the short growing season, low light conditions, and lack of nutrients in the tundra, few plants could carry out the life cycle of an annual successfully every growing season.

**Self-sufficient Seeds**   By forming seeds, tundra plants spread to new areas and increase genetic diversity. But in order to produce seeds, most plants must be fertilized by pollen from another plant. Most tundra plants have pollen that is carried from one plant to another by wind. Some are pollinated by insects, such as flies and mosquitoes.

**March of the Clones**   Seeds aren't the only way to create new plants. Sedges, grasses, and arctic willows produce underground and aboveground stems that "reach out" and form new, separate plants. Unlike the plants that grow from seeds, these new plants are clones: they are genetically identical to the original plant.

### THE BEST SPOTS TO GROW

Tundra plants make the most of very little: very little warmth, very little time to grow, and very few nutrients in the soil. As a result, any small change in these conditions can make a big difference in an individual plant's growth.

**Owl Mounds**   It's no coincidence that tall, showy plants such as larkspur and monkshood grow thick on the raised mounds where snowy owls perch. Owl droppings and pellets act as fertilizer, giving the soil a nutrient boost that encourages lush plant growth. Plants also grow thick around lemming burrows and fox dens, where animal droppings fertilize the soil. So if you're looking for a lemming burrow, look in the places with lush plants!

**Mini-greenhouses**   Some plants' growth is speeded up by natural "hothouses" in the snow. These spots form when sun shining through the snow warms the dark soil. The lower snow layers near this warm soil melt, leaving a space—a tiny dome in the snow. The upper layer of snow, partly melted on the inside, then refreezes, forming an icy window. Once formed, this natural cavity acts like a greenhouse; sun shining through the ice warms the soil and the air inside. Heat builds up, and this little cavity may become 18°F (10°C) warmer than the outside air. Chickweed, cinquefoil, saxifrage, and poppies that happen to grow in these pockets can be far along in their development by the time the snow and ice melts and other plants just begin to sprout.

### PLANT LOOK-ALIKE

What thing, neither plant nor animal, grows in some of the coldest, most windswept places in the world? Lichen. You've probably seen lichen somewhere, its gray-white, brown, or green flaky mats growing on trees, rocks, or gravestones. Or perhaps you've seen its red-topped stalks, which are nicknamed British soldiers.

These plantlike growths are not one organism, but at least two: an alga and a fungus. The fungus, the main structure of lichen, supports and protects the algae within its tissues. (Fungi are not plants, as many people believe. They belong to their own kingdom, the kingdom Fungi.) The alga, a plant, produces food the fungus can use to live. This relationship is mutualistic, because both partners, in this case the alga and the fungus, benefit from the arrangement. When wet, lichen can be leathery and strong, forming a tough mat. Yet it is also delicate; when dry it crumbles

*This close-up shows the stalks of one particular lichen:
British soldier. Tundra lichens vary in appearance.*

and crunches underfoot. And it's slow-growing and easily damaged by air pollution.

Reindeer moss, a favorite food of reindeer, is not a moss, but a lichen. Reindeer paw away the tundra snow to find this nutritious food underneath. They may eat nothing but lichen for the entire winter.

# ❋5❋
# TUNDRA ANIMALS

Like plants, tundra animals have a seasonal rhythm to their lives. In spring, gyrfalcons switch from a diet of ptarmigans to a diet of lemmings. In summer, snow geese raise their young. In fall, brown bears settle down for a long winter's nap. Cold weather has a lot to do with these animals' seasonal activities. But much of their behavior is more directly linked to the availability of food. Food supply, in turn, depends on plant and animal life cycles that are influenced by day length, snow cover, and cold weather. All these factors play a role in setting the tempo of tundra animals' lives.

## RESIDENTS AND VISITORS

Some animals don't have to deal with the tundra's cold, dark winter days. Millions of ducks, geese, loons, gulls, and sandpipers live in the tundra only in spring and summer. These birds are visitors from the south, taking advantage of choice nesting spots and a summertime bounty of insects and plants in the tundra. Other migrants include caribou, which trek thousands of miles from the taiga to the tundra where they graze on summer plants and bear calves.

**The World's Greatest Traveler**   A tundra visitor called the arctic tern carries out the longest migration of any creature on earth—a more than 22,000-mile (36,000-kilometer) trip from the Arctic to the Antarctic and back, each year. This

*The arctic tern, commonly seen hovering over tundra ponds, migrates from the Arctic to the Antarctic and back, farther than any other creature on earth.*

strenuous journey gives the tern the best of two worlds, and more daylight per year than any other species. Each summer it nests and feeds in the Arctic. Then it travels to the Antarctic, reaching it just in time to take advantage of its summer, which also features 24-hour sunlit days and an abundance of food.

**Those Hardy Residents**   After the summer "crowds" have left, only a few animal species remain on the tundra. Those that stay around for the winter months include willow ptarmigans, snow buntings, brown bears, arctic foxes, arctic ground squirrels, ravens, snowy owls, and a variety of insects. But even among these creatures, there are few that remain fully active in the winter. Beneath the snow, many tundra creatures reduce or practically cease activity during the cold.

# · THE GREAT MIGRATION ·

Now that most of the buffalo are gone, the yearly trek of the caribou is the last great migration of herd animals left in North America. In the eighteenth and nineteenth centuries, explorers saw mile-wide herds of millions of caribou that often took days to pass by. Today these herds number only in the hundreds of thousands, but the spectacle of their migration is still impressive. In a year, a single caribou may travel 2,700 miles (4,400 kilometers).

Several large herds exist in Alaska and northern Canada. The Porcupine caribou herd, which is named after the Porcupine River, travels in spring from the taiga in Canada and south of the Brooks Mountain Range in the United States, to its calving grounds on the coastal plain of Alaska. The females, called cows, go first. A month later the males, called bulls, arrive. After the young are born, the herd breaks up into small groups that scatter, grazing on the tundra's summer growth. In fall the caribou regroup near the taiga for mating season, where bulls battle one another using their racks of antlers.

During their long migrations, caribou are not alone. Wolf packs follow close behind, working in groups to hunt them. During summer, billions of mosquitoes plague the caribou. In just one week, a caribou may lose four pints (almost two liters) of blood to these and other biting insects. At their calving grounds, young caribou may fall prey to bears or wolverines as well as wolves. Many Arctic people also hunt the caribou, eating their meat and using their hides for clothing.

The reindeer of Scandinavia and the caribou of North America are the same species, although they live in different areas. Generally, however, people call the domesticated or semi-domesticated animals in Europe reindeer, while the wild ones in Alaska and Canada are referred to as caribou.

# BEATING THE CHILL

You might think snow would be harmful to animals. But in fact, snow is the key to winter survival for lemmings, voles, weasels, hares, and lots of other small, furry creatures. These animals dig burrows and tunnel networks beneath the snow, which is topped by a rigid, snow-and-ice crust called hoarfrost. Just 10 inches (25 centimeters) down under the blanket of snow, temperatures remain fairly constant, around freezing. For extra warmth, lemmings line their tunnels with grass. Cozy under the snow, they can dig for plants to eat, and even mate and raise young in midwinter. They're among the most active animals in winter.

**Winter Sleep**  Unlike lemmings, many animals that snuggle under the snow don't remain active. Arctic ground squirrels hibernate. This means they spend the winter in a sluggish or motionless state, with reduced body function and a lowered body temperature that may be close to freezing. By remaining in this state during the winter, ground squirrels save energy, reducing their need for food and water, which helps them survive until spring when food and unfrozen water are more plentiful.

Bears, which are famous for hibernating, actually do not hibernate, according to most scientists. During their winter denning period, bears are too active, wake up too quickly, and have too high a body temperature to qualify as true hibernators. During that time they even give birth to cubs!

**Wild and Woolly**  One of the few tundra animals that doesn't seek protection from winter storms is the musk ox. This tundra native is small and stocky with long, warm fur. A strand of its fur can be as much as three feet (nearly a meter) long! The musk ox's shaggy coat has two layers: long, black protective hair on the outside with soft, warm

*Even harsh winters do not bother musk oxen, which are well-adapted to the tundra environment.*

underfur in a layer beneath. In summer, musk oxen shed this underfur; some Arctic peoples collect it and knit it into clothing. These animals are so well-insulated that they can lie down and take a nap on hard-packed snow without even melting the snow beneath them!

**Solar Collectors** Tundra animals, such as ptarmigans and ground squirrels, save energy by using solar heating. Ptarmigans perch on prominent branches to warm up in the morning sun. Arctic ground squirrels shift from patches of sun to shady spots to warm up and cool off during the summer. And tundra insects, even butterflies, tend to be small, dark, and hairy. Dark color helps them to warm up quickly in the sun, and hair helps to trap that warmth against their outer surfaces. Small size helps them warm up quickly, too. Nevertheless, some scientists believe tundra insects' small size may be more a result of Arctic food shortages than an adaptation for warming.

**Antifreeze** For Arctic creatures, freezing is a real danger. When body fluids freeze inside cells, they expand, forming ice crystals that can burst cell walls. To combat this danger, some insects dehydrate in winter so there will be less body fluid to freeze. Other insects build up antifreeze agents that lower the freezing point of their body fluids. This makes them more resistant to freezing.

**Supercooling** Yet another strategy for preventing freezing is supercooling. Supercooled animals have body fluids that get below the freezing point without freezing solid. That's because these fluids have very few ice nuclei. To form, ice needs a nucleus—a bit of dirt, dust, or other substance—on which its crystal can grow. Supercooled insects and ground squirrels clear their systems of most of the substances that might act as ice nuclei. So, very little of their body fluid freezes. Many insects use a combination of antifreeze, super-cooling, and other strategies to survive the tundra winter.

**Allen's Rule** Allen's rule, named for American zoologist Joel Asaph Allen, states that animals that live in colder regions of the earth have smaller appendages—arms, legs, ears, and other parts that stick out from the body—than species that live in hotter regions. For example, the ears of an arctic fox are much smaller than those of a desert fox. The tail of an arctic lemming is shorter than the tail of lemmings farther south. Allen's rule makes sense because for animals in colder climates, big ears, long legs, or a long tail would be a real frostbite risk. It's difficult for an animal to pump enough warmed blood into its extremities to keep them warm. But animals in warm climates may benefit from larger appendages, which can cool the blood pumped through them.

### MEALTIME IN THE TUNDRA

Even in the tundra, there's more to staying alive than just staying warm. With strong paws, digging claws, and even tiny insect jaws, tundra animals find food. By a variety of other methods, they must also avoid becoming a meal themselves. Below are three of the many techniques tundra animals use to survive.

**Seasonal Change**   Having a variable diet is one way animals adjust to the tundra's seasonal food supply. Caribou eat many different plants in summer, but in the winter live almost entirely on lichen they find by digging down in the snow with their hooves. Gyrfalcons eat ptarmigans, hares, and snow buntings in winter, but in summer they eat a wider variety of prey, including lemmings and squirrels. In summer, brown bears dine on berries and salmon; but in spring, when food choices are few, they may dig up roots, or even eat seaweed along the shore.

**Fitting In**   How do you find a ptarmigan in a snowy winter landscape? You don't. Ptarmigans' white feathers fit in so well with the snow that they're hard to see. In summer, these birds molt their white feathers and grow dappled brown ones that match the landscape. This adaptation is called camouflage. Camouflage helps ptarmigans hide from gyrfalcons, foxes, weasels, and other predators who'd make them into a meal. But camouflage can also work for predators, hiding them as they sneak up on prey. Short-tailed weasels, snowy owls, and arctic foxes are white or light-colored in winter and darker-colored in summer.

**Bodyguards**   To protect their young, adult musk oxen form a circle facing outward, with babies in the middle. They create a shoulder-to-shoulder line of defense that helps deter wolves. Unfortunately, in the past this defense proved useless against human predators, who simply shot all the musk oxen within minutes. In the 1800s the entire Alaskan population of this species was wiped out by European hunters. Today musk oxen from other areas are

*An arctic fox with its winter-white fur can be hard to spot against a background of snow.*

being bred and protected, and they have been reintroduced to the Alaskan tundra.

## FAMILY LIFE

There's more to an animal's life than keeping warm, finding food, and evading predators. Animals also need to attract mates, establish territories, and raise young.

**Headgear** Sometimes they're used for territorial battles, but antlers also help caribou and moose attract mates. Grown and shed yearly, caribou and moose antlers are made of bone. In spring and summer, a capillary-filled layer called velvet covers the antlers, bringing blood to help grow the bone. In fall, when the antlers are fully developed, this layer is shed and the bony antlers revealed. In most deer species, such as moose, only the males have antlers. Both male and female caribou have antlers, but only the males sport larger, many-branched racks. The size of a male's antlers indicates its genetic and physical health. Each year, after mating season, these antlers are shed. New ones are grown the next year.

**Race Against Time**    Mating, laying eggs or giving birth, and raising young aren't easy in the short tundra summer. If the snow melts late, as it sometimes does, animals whose young need longer to develop may be crunched for time. As a result, nest space is definitely at a premium in early spring, when snow is just melting on the tundra. Rough-legged hawks, peregrine falcons, and snowy owls may be seen nesting peacefully right beside geese. That's very surprising considering these hawks, falcons, and owls usually eat other birds! Apparently these avian predators are so occupied with family duties that they don't generally bother the geese.

## WIDE-RANGING SPECIES

With all the amazing adaptations discussed in this chapter, tundra animals might seem uniquely suited for the tundra life. In some ways they are. Yet many of these creatures, such as the caribou, wolf, and brown bear also range south into taiga forests. Part of the reason for this is that the tundra is a young biome; it has only been around for 10,000 years or so. With the exception of the musk oxen, which survived the last ice age in the Arctic, animals moved up from other biomes into the tundra as the ice retreated thousands of years ago. So it's natural many would still range into the taiga farther south.

# ❋6❋
# TUNDRA COMMUNITIES

Tundra animals and plants don't adapt just to cold conditions and a short growing and breeding season. Over thousands of years, they have adapted to one another, forming tightly woven communities. Scientists who study these communities and their relationship to the physical environment are called ecologists.

## GOING WITH THE FLOW

Energy flow is what links together the animals and plants in a community. In the tundra, for instance, energy in the form of sunlight is used by a cotton grass plant to make sugars, which are stored as starch in its leaves, roots, and shoots. When these plant parts are eaten by a lemming, some of the energy in them becomes part of the lemming. Some of the energy is lost as heat, as it is at every step of the process. So, when a fox eats the lemming, only part of the energy in its body becomes part of the fox.

When the fox dies, decomposers and scavengers eat its body, and some of the fox's energy becomes part of them. The leftovers and by-products of their meal become part of the soil. In warm biomes, such as the tropics, this decomposition can happen very quickly. But decomposition occurs very slowly in the tundra, partly because it is cold much of the year.

**Energetic Ideas**   A simple diagram of energy links such as the ones described above is called a food chain. Several food chains, linked together, create a food web—a diagram ecologists use to show the energy relationships among many organisms in a community. In general, tundra food chains are shorter and tundra food webs are simpler than those in other biomes. They are shorter and simpler because so few species of animals and plants inhabit the tundra.

**The Energy Crisis**   It seems in every biome there's some limiting factor—something that limits the growth of plants and animals. In the desert, it's water. In rain forests, it's generally nutrients. In the tundra, it's energy that's lacking, though nutrients may be missing, too. Because of their position on the earth, polar regions such as the tundra receive less solar energy than places closer to the equator. And the shiny snow, ice, and pond surfaces in these regions reflect back much of the solar energy that does arrive. As a result, the tundra is on a tight energy budget. Its entire community relies on less energy than communities in other biomes do.

## PREDATORS, PYRAMIDS, AND POPULATIONS

It takes more than one lemming to satisfy an arctic fox's appetite. And each lemming eats more than one plant to survive. But these aren't just eating habits; they're a reflection of how much energy flows through a community, and where it goes. To express these energy quantities, ecologists use an energy pyramid. In a general way, the pyramid shows how many producers—plants—are needed to feed the primary consumers—lemmings—that are needed to feed the secondary consumer (also called a predator)—an arctic fox. At each level of the pyramid, energy is lost, so it takes more energy, in the form of animals, to feed the top predator on the pyramid. Looking at such a pyramid, you can see why the tundra needs to have more lemmings than arctic foxes. And since gyrfalcons, snowy owls, wolves, and other predators also eat lemmings, you can see why you would really need *lots* of lemmings to support all these predators!

**Lots of Lemmings**  Even with gyrfalcons, owls, wolves, and foxes snacking on them, lemmings can still reproduce so quickly that their populations explode dramatically. A mature female lemming can produce eight litters of four to five young a year. Every three to six years the lemming population grows so big that even the predators don't eat enough to keep their numbers down. When this happens, the lemmings become frenzied and hyperactive. They run in all directions, over the tundra, the snow, and the ice. If they reach a stream, pond, or river, they'll run along the edge, or jump in and swim across.

**The Myth of the Lemmings**  Often lemmings drown in large rivers or the ocean, when they jump in and try to swim across. This behavior is what gave rise to the myth that lemmings run down to the sea and jump in to commit suicide. Actually, the lemmings are just spreading out, like locusts that build up in numbers then travel in swarms to new areas. The year after a peak population year, very few lemmings remain on the tundra.

**Predator–Prey Cycles**  Either way, the rise and fall of lemming populations has a noticeable impact on the tundra predators who eat them. If lemmings are plentiful, foxes, weasels, skuas, owls, jaegers, and other predator populations increase soon after. But when lemming populations crash, predators go hungry. Soon young pups and chicks die, and predator populations decline, too.

*Lemming populations peak and crash in a fairly regular cycle.*

## THE MEASURES OF LIFE

If you took all the plants in a square mile of tundra and piled them up on a scale, how much would they all weigh? It's hard to say. Yet this is the kind of thing ecologists try to measure, at least for small areas. The weight of plant matter—roots, shoots, and other parts—for a certain area is called plant biomass. Ecologists use biomass figures to compare the productivity of biomes. In general, tundras are much less productive than other biomes, except for hot deserts and polar deserts.

**Diversity** Another important measure of a biome is species diversity. Species diversity is how many different kinds of animals and plants live in a place. Rain forests have lots of different kinds of plants and animals; an extremely high species diversity. But the tundra has a very low species diversity. For instance, only 50 of the earth's 4,000 mammal species live in Arctic regions.

## FOREST–TUNDRA: A LAND IN BETWEEN

Where the green forests of the taiga end, the treeless land of the tundra doesn't suddenly begin. In between is a zone called the forest–tundra. The forest–tundra is an ecotone, a transition area between two biomes. Here the biomes' plants and animals overlap, mix and mingle, making a special habitat all their own.

In the forest–tundra ecotone, trees grow in patches, with short shrubs or grass in between. White and black spruce that grow very tall in the forest may reach heights of only a few feet here. Short and stunted, their branches grow out along the ground, forming wide skirts of greenery. This low-growing tree shape is called krummholz. These trees can be several hundred years old, yet only a few feet tall.

## A TASTE OF THE TUNDRA

To really experience Arctic tundra, you should visit the Arctic regions in northern Alaska, Canada, Greenland, Scandinavia, or Siberia. But if you live farther south, you still may be able to get a taste of what a tundra is like, a little closer to home. By climbing a high mountain, you can reach altitudes where climatic conditions are somewhat similar to places hundreds, even thousands of miles north. These high altitude spots harbor alpine tundra—the remnants of a type of tundra that once stretched farther south of where it exists today.

**Some Similarities**   Hiking up a mountain in the Colorado Rockies, the Cascades, or even in New England, you can hike through taiga, then alpine tundra. Alpine tundra has a lot in common with Arctic tundra. It has a summer carpet of low-growing plants with colorful flowers that attract insects. Bears roam, ground squirrels scurry, and even ptarmigans thrive in alpine tundra just as they do in the

Arctic tundra. And many of the plants—mosses, saxifrages, buttercups, and others—are the same species as in the Arctic tundra.

## TAKE A HIKE IN THE ARCTIC TUNDRA

In summer, hiking on the marshy, lumpy ground of the Arctic tundra can be slow going. Good boots come in handy. If there isn't a wind, then long pants, long sleeves, and mosquito repellent or a mosquito net for your head wouldn't be a bad idea to keep off the bugs. Weather can turn quickly; snowfall isn't unheard-of in June. So it's best to be prepared for inclement weather and emergencies, especially since there usually aren't many people around and you may have to rely on your own supplies. Most park services and wilderness outfitters can let you know how to prepare. As always, know where you're going, tell someone of your plans, and bring enough food and water to keep your energy level high.

Be sure to bring binoculars, too. You can use them to observe waterfowl nesting, or brown bears from a safe distance. And if you turn the binoculars around and look through the wide end, you can use them as a magnifier to look at tiny tundra plants close-up.

Here are just a few of the things you can look for and listen for on an Arctic tundra hike:

- Insects resting inside tundra flowers;
- Tiny leaves of tundra plants;
- Fluffy tops of cotton grass blossoms;
- Nests of sanderlings on the ground;
- The call of wolves;
- Ptarmigans warming up in the morning sun;
- The fuzzy catkins—buds—of willows;
- Large holes where bears have dug up ground squirrels;

- Wide hoofprints of caribou;
- The honking of geese flying overhead;
- The courting dances of nesting migrant birds;
- Long, snaking walls of dirt—the eskers left by retreating glaciers;
- Antlers shed last season;
- Squiggling insect larvae in ponds;
- Snowy owls gliding down on lemmings.

**Important Differences**   There are differences between alpine and Arctic tundra. Because it is closer to the equator, alpine tundra receives more direct sunlight than Arctic tundra. Day and night cycles differ from Arctic tundra. And temperatures fluctuate more widely and more often than in Arctic tundra. Alpine areas also get more rainfall than Arctic tundra, but because they are generally well drained, they aren't as soggy as Arctic tundra. Finally, compared to the complex mosaic of wet and dry spots in the Arctic tundra, alpine tundra is somewhat simpler and more uniform.

## TUNDRA THROUGH THE AGES

The Arctic tundra is a young biome, newly revealed by ice caps that receded after the last ice age, about 10,000 years ago. As the earth warmed, ice caps melted and shrank. Plants spread over the newly revealed ground, and animals who ate the plants, such as reindeer, moved north to colonize this land.

Before that time, a grassland similar to the tundra had existed much farther south. But with the earth's warming, these areas became forested. Only a little of this grassland tundra was left, on high mountains where conditions were still cold. These are the alpine tundra regions of today. Many of the cold-adapted plants of these alpine regions spread north and helped colonize the tundra. They helped make the Arctic what it is today.

# ☀7☀
# PEOPLE AND
# THE TUNDRA

The Dindye of Fort Yukon, Alaska, have a word for it: *det-thlo(k)*. That's snow deep enough to need snowshoes. The Inuit of Kobuk Valley, Alaska, speak of *api*—snow on the ground, *siqoq*—drifting snow, and *qali*—snow that collects on trees. With one word these Arctic people can say what it takes an English speaker several words to describe. Perhaps that is because Arctic people live in a snowy world where such terms come in handy. No one can say. What is certain, however, is that knowing the environment, and heeding its cues, has helped Arctic people survive and thrive in icy lands for thousands of years.

Today snowmobiles, airplanes, and other modern inventions make Arctic life a little easier for some residents. But these technologies, and the influx of people into Arctic regions, have increased environmental stress on fragile tundra lands and brought cultural change for Arctic people. How to deal with these forces of change is one of the major challenges for the future.

## ANCIENT TUNDRA PEOPLE
The first people to come to North America crossed over the Bering Land Bridge, in a region called Beringia. This land bridge existed several times in the past 40,000 years, whenever the climate was cold enough to lock up much of the ocean's water in ice, thereby lowering the sea and exposing

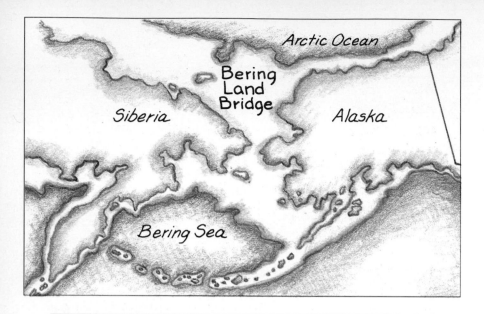

*Beringia is the name given to the regions of Siberia and Alaska once connected by a land bridge.*

Beringia's land. At times the sea was so low, there was a 1,000-mile- (1,600-kilometer- ) wide link between what is now Alaska and the region of Russia called Siberia.

Anthropologists, who study the history of humans, aren't sure exactly when people crossed over from Asia to North America. But it must have happened sometime between 11,000 and 40,000 years ago. The first people—the American Indians—crossed the bridge and went south. When the last ice age ended, some of these people returned north, perhaps following the caribou that grazed on lands newly revealed by the ice. Then, about 10,000 years ago, another group of people migrated from Asia and settled in North America. These were the Inuit. Much later, by boat, the Inuit colonized islands in the Canadian Archipelago. (In the past, the Inuit were often called "Eskimo," a word that comes from an Algonquin Indian term meaning "eaters of raw meat." They prefer the name "Inuit," which in their language means "the People.")

Today many native groups—the Saami, Chukchi, Aleuts, Inuits, and others—inhabit the circumpolar Arctic. Although cultural practices vary, their hunting and gathering habits are quite similar. Most harvest berries, herbs, lemmings, freshwater fish, and caribou from the tundra, but rely in large part on ocean resources such as whales, seals, walrus, and saltwater fish. For most of their history, these people, without the technology to make metal, fashioned knives, spears, and sewing needles from bone and ivory.

**More than Just Survival**   Human life in the Arctic involves more than just mere survival. Over the years, Arctic people have developed a complex and rich culture, which involves singing, storytelling, and dancing. These arts help them entertain on cold Arctic nights, teach their children, and honor the spirits of the world around them. Their religion involves both prayer and sacrifices of food to honor the spirits in the caribou, the whale, the river, the sky—all of the natural world.

## THE WINDS OF CHANGE

For thousands of years, the lives of the people in the Arctic remained virtually unchanged. But in the 1700s and 1800s European, Canadian, and later American whaling boats moved into the Arctic to hunt whales and other wildlife on land and in the sea. These hunters wiped out the Alaskan population of musk oxen and the world's population of the Steller's sea cow—a relative of the Florida manatee. By 1914, the hunting frenzy in Alaska had killed off millions of seals, reduced a population of 20,000 bowhead whales to 1,000, and cut the nearby walrus population by 85 percent. So much of the wildlife was gone, the hunters from outside the Arctic left. But by then the Inuit people's lives had been permanently changed. Outsiders had killed off wild game the Inuit depended on, and had brought disease, liquor, gambling, and new technology to their lives. The Inuit population had already decreased by one-half.

After World War II, to keep an eye on the Soviet Union and prepare for possible war, the United States established military bases on Alaska's Arctic tundra. This brought new people to the area. Then, in the late 1960s, the discovery of oil on Alaska's North Slope spurred more development. New towns were created almost overnight, to house the people who were needed to set up and run the machinery that pumped and transported oil. These changes, and government regulations requiring formal schooling for children, also caused Alaska's native people—who had formerly been migratory—to settle into towns.

## PEOPLE IN THE TUNDRA TODAY

Although some Arctic people live a completely traditional lifestyle, most live a life that is a combination of old and new. Natives of Alaska may live in wooden or concrete houses most of the year, but sleep in skin or cloth tents when out hunting. Children go to school, but learn their native language in addition to English. At home, kids may eat pizza, but also enjoy muktuk—an Inuit delicacy of whale skin and blubber. And although Inuit kids may watch television and play basketball, they may also spend time listening to their elders' traditional stories and learning their culture's dances.

**Native Rights**  Many Arctic people traditionally wandered far and wide as part of their lifestyle, so they consider large areas to be their hunting grounds. But when outsiders moved into the Arctic, they wanted the land carved up into plots that individuals could own. For years, land disputes raged. In 1971, the United States government settled with

*On the tundra in Barrow, Alaska, kids play softball, as they do in almost every North American biome.*

Alaska's native residents, allocating large tracts of land to native corporations in which the natives received shares. Each shareholder was required to keep his or her stock for a certain number of years, but then they could sell. Many people fear that when the deadline arrives, individuals will sell their shares and the native groups as a whole will lose the unity of their ancestral lands.

## OIL: THE PROMISES AND THE PROBLEMS

Oil is a big business in Alaska. On tundra at the edge of the Arctic Ocean, oil rigs and trucks dot the gigantic oil fields near Prudhoe Bay. The 800-mile- (1,290-kilometer- ) long Alaskan pipeline takes that oil from Prudhoe to the south-central coast of Alaska, where it is loaded into tankers in Prince William Sound, the site of the catastrophic *Exxon Valdez* oil spill in March 1989.

Many people in Alaska and Canada profit from the oil industry. But not everyone is happy with it. Oil spills and development of oil drilling facilities can hurt hunting and fishing, which are also important industries. Oil drilling involves building roads, processing facilities, airstrips, and housing for workers, and inevitably destroys tundra. In addition to these negative impacts, oil drilling can disrupt the activities of wildlife in the area. Processing facilities produce huge black clouds of air pollution that form a haze over the tundra, and drilling produces large quantities of hazardous waste that are stored in open pits on the tundra.

**Drilling Controversies**   Over the past few years, oil companies have pushed the United States Congress to allow oil drilling in new areas. The main site of controversy is Alaska's Arctic National Wildlife Refuge, which is believed to have a large oil reservoir underneath it. The Arctic National Wildlife Refuge is one of the last great wildernesses left on earth—an expanse of tundra where wolves, bears, musk oxen, and caribou roam, and where many of these animals raise their young. Environmentalists fervently defend it.

Oil companies argue that drilling in the Arctic National Wildlife Refuge will provide jobs for thousands of people and decrease the United States' reliance on foreign oil. They also say that drilling operations will not significantly damage the tundra. Defenders of the area disagree. They say that drilling there will provide only a fraction of the oil the United States needs. They also argue that even moderate energy conservation efforts in the United States could save as much oil as would be produced by drilling oil in the Arctic National Wildlife Refuge. Environmentalists also point out that one day soon the world will run out of oil reserves and have to switch to other energy sources. They propose that we investigate these alternative energy sources and start using them now, *before* resorting to drilling in one of North America's last wildernesses.

## GLOBAL WARMING AND THE
## GREENHOUSE EFFECT

The greenhouse effect is a natural process, not a modern invention. Up in the atmosphere are billions of molecules of carbon dioxide and other naturally occurring greenhouse gases. These gases act like the glass panes of a greenhouse, allowing sunlight into the earth's atmosphere, but allowing only some of the sunlight-generated heat to escape. These gases keep the earth warm.

The problem today is that the quantity of these gases in the atmosphere has gone way up, especially in the last 100 years. Much of this extra gas comes from people's activities—cattle ranching, industrial plants, automobiles, and the burning of tropical forests. But natural sources such as volcanoes and wetlands also give off greenhouse gases.

Scientists aren't sure exactly how all this greenhouse gas will change the earth's climate. But they are fairly sure changes are going to happen within the next 50 years. And whatever happens, these changes will have a drastic impact on the lives of people all over the earth.

A majority of scientists believe these gases will cause global warming—a rise in the earth's temperature of several degrees. This change will likely impact the Arctic and Antarctic more drastically than any other regions of the earth. This warming is expected to melt the polar ice caps, raising sea levels around the world, and flooding low-lying coastal areas.

In the Arctic, warmer temperatures will melt snow cover, prolong the snow-free season, melt part of the permafrost, and flood some coastal areas. The solid ice the Arctic animals walk across to get from island to island will be gone. This could isolate these islands, drastically affecting wildlife populations there. Over hundreds of years, this climate change could cause forests to spread farther north. But all in all, the results of global warming for the tundra and nearby regions are complex and uncertain. Whether or not the earth warms, as many suspect, or it cools, as some others predict, the buildup of these greenhouse gases will have global implications that will damage plants, animals, and people who rely on and have adapted to conditions on certain parts of the globe.

## OTHER CONSERVATION THREATS
## TO THE TUNDRA

Tundra regions are still only sparsely populated. Certainly, the people there have an impact on their environment. But for the most part, conservation threats to the tundra come not from within it, but from outside it—from the people who live in other biomes. What happens to Arctic lands depends on outside factors as diverse as the price of oil set by oil cartels in the Middle East, to the safety of power plants in Russia, and the decision of a woman in Atlanta to turn on her air conditioning.

Here, in brief, are the main factors, besides oil drilling and global climate change, that can have a negative impact on tundra ecology:

**Ozone Depletion**   Over the last few years, the earth's ozone layer has thinned, especially over the North and South Poles. The thinning of the ozone layer, which protects the earth from much of the sun's harmful radiation, is the suspected cause behind the worldwide rise in skin cancer rates. It is unknown what other effects this increased ultraviolet radiation will have on plants and animals of the tundra. Chlorofluorocarbons (CFCs) and other chemicals people use to make aerosol foam and to run refrigerators are destroying the ozone layer.

**Air Pollution**   Pollution from Russian and Eastern European factories, and to a lesser degree factories in the eastern

United States, can be carried by wind to the tundra. Here it forms a haze of smog. In 1986, radioactive particles from the explosion of the Chernobyl nuclear power plant in the Soviet Union spread over Scandinavia, including the homelands of the Saami people. This radiation contaminated lichen and other plants reindeer eat. In turn, it poisoned the reindeer, a major source of food for the Saami. The sale of reindeer meat was banned. Crops were also contaminated and had to be discarded. Air pollution from local Arctic sources, such as cars, wood burning, industry, and other activities can also build up and be trapped close to the ground by temperature inversions common in the Arctic. And lichen, a staple of many tundra animals' diet, is easily killed by air pollution.

**Development**   Like all other biomes, unwise development could spoil many tundra lands. At present, the human population of the tundra is still sparse. But future development could put the tundra and its wildlife in jeopardy, through habitat loss and habitat degradation because of pollution.

**Mining**   Mining for gold and other minerals is widespread in tundra regions. Chemicals used in mining can contaminate streams, and the process as a whole can leave scars upon the land.

**Overhunting**   Hunting and fishing are an important and sacred part of native culture. The meat gained from hunting and fishing is still the mainstay of the diet of many native people and recent immigrants to tundra lands. But today guns, powerboats, planes, and snowmobiles make hunting easier. From all over the world, sport hunters and fishermen come to tundra areas to hunt bears, wolves, moose, elk, and other animals, and to fish for salmon and other delicacies. These tourists bring much needed money to remote

Alaskan and Canadian people. But with the increased hunting pressure, some wildlife managers are beginning to wonder if more restrictive regulations on hunting will be needed in the future.

## HOPE FOR THE FUTURE

There's a saying in Russia: "There's no bad weather, only bad clothing." This is the kind of hardy, cold-tolerant attitude that has helped Arctic people survive in a harsh environment for thousands of years. And it may be the kind of positive attitude Arctic people will need to get through the challenges they face.

Over the past few years, the approach to environmental issues in the Arctic has changed somewhat. Environmental groups, once working mostly on their own, now find allies, working in concert with groups of native peoples such as the Gwich'in Athabascan people of the United States and Canada, and the Saami of Scandinavia. By recognizing the needs and rights of these native peoples and the environmental problems in the Arctic, they are trying to come up with solutions that satisfy many groups. Here are some of the specific things people in the Arctic, and around the world, are doing to preserve tundra lands and tundra cultures:

- Environmental and Native American groups are lobbying Congress to designate parts of Alaska's Arctic National Wildlife Refuge as a wilderness area. This designation would make these areas, which include the Porcupine caribou herd's calving grounds, off-limits to oil drilling.
- Aulavik National Park, which protects important habitat for musk oxen and caribou, was established in 1992 by the government of Canada, working with the local native people.
- In June 1990, Presidents George Bush and Mikhail Gorbachev agreed to establish a cooperative international

park, the Beringia International Heritage Park. This park would include the tundra lands of the Bering Land Bridge in both countries.

- Coalitions of scientists from the United States and Europe are meeting with people in Russia and other former Soviet countries to exchange information on new technologies available for cleaner, safer running of industrial plants. Their efforts might help clean up Arctic air pollution.
- A new organization called the Arctic Network has been established to coordinate the work of environmental non-profit groups and native groups from the eight Arctic countries: Denmark, Canada, Finland, Sweden, Russia, Iceland, the United States, and Norway.
- Environmental activists are writing letters, making phone calls, and talking to local and national legislators about preserving wetlands. Much of the Arctic tundra is dotted by ponds and is considered wetland.

With so many people working to help protect the tundra, the future for this biome looks bright, but still full of challenges. So no matter where you live, there's plenty of room for you to join in the global effort to preserve the Arctic tundra.

# RESOURCES AND WHAT
# YOU CAN DO TO HELP

❧

Here's what you can do to help ensure that tundras are conserved:

• Learn more by reading books and watching videos and television programs about the tundra. Check your local library, bookstore, and video store for resources. Here are just a few of the books available for further reading:

*Arctic Hunter* by Diane Hoyt-Goldsmith (Holiday House, 1992).
*The Arctic World Series,* a four-book series by Bobbie Kalman (Crabtree, 1988).
*In Two Worlds*: *A Yup'ik Eskimo Family* by Aylette Jeness and Alice Rivers, (Houghton Mifflin, 1989).
*Julie of the Wolves,* by Jean Craighead George (Harper & Row, 1972).
"Peoples of the Arctic," by Joseph Judge (*National Geographic,* February 1983).

• For more information on tundra and tundra-related issues, write or call the following organizations:

**Audubon Society**
Alaska Regional Office
308 G Street #217
Anchorage, AK 99501
Phone 1-907-278-3007

**Northern Alaska Environmental Center**
218 Driveway Street
Fairbanks, AK 99701
Phone 1-907-452-5021

**Wilderness Society Regional Office**
430 West 7th Avenue
Suite 210
Anchorage, AK 99501-3550
Phone 1-907-272-9453

You may also want to join these organizations and support their efforts.

•Visit a museum, national park, national monument, or botanical garden that has tundra features or displays. The following North American parks, refuges, and national monuments contain Arctic tundra:

Canada
**Aulavik National Park,** Sachs Harbor, NT
**Auyuittuq National Park,** Pangnirtung, NT
**Ellesmere Island National Park Reserve,** Grise Fiord, NT
**Ivvavik (also called Northern Yukon National Park),**
   Inuvik, NT
**Polar Bear Pass National Wildlife Area,** Resolute, NT

United States
**Alaska Maritime National Wildlife Refuge,** Homer, AK
**Arctic National Wildlife Refuge,** Fairbanks, AK
**Bering Land Bridge National Preserve,** AK
**Gates of the Arctic National Park and Preserve,**
   Fairbanks, AK
**Yukon Delta National Wildlife Refuge,** Bethel, AK

• Conserve oil so that fewer tundra areas will have to be developed for oil drilling. Here are some oil-saving tips:

• • Walk, bike, or use public transportation—buses and trains—whenever possible. Organize a carpool to places you must go to by car.

• • Recycle aluminum cans, paper, plastic, and other products. Recycling uses less energy than making a product from scratch. Also, buy recycled products. For a catalog of recycled products, contact:

**Earth Care Paper, Inc.**
200 Clara Street
Ukiah, CA 95482-8507
Phone 1-800-347-0070

- • Turn off lights, televisions, and other appliances when you are not using them. Saving electricity can save oil because some power plants generate electricity by burning oil. For more energy-saving tips, contact your local electric utility.

- • Ask others to be car smart. Encourage them not to speed because speeding wastes gas. Also, cars that are tuned up, with properly inflated tires, waste less gas. Used motor oil should be taken to a filling station to be recycled.

- • Encourage your family to use energy-saving devices in your home. For a catalog of energy-saving appliances and other environmental products, contact:

**Real Goods**
966 Mazzoni Street
Ukiah, CA 95482-3471
Phone 1-800-762-7325

**Seventh Generation**
Colchester, VT
05446-1672
Phone 1-800-456-1177

- Educate others about the tundra and Arctic people. Put on a skit at school, construct a display for the hall or a mall, or sponsor a wolf walkathon to raise awareness of issues. You could also discuss Arctic people, and the conservation threats facing the tundra.

- Write letters to state and national government officials, telling them you feel tundra conservation is important.

# GLOSSARY

✳

**active layer**   a layer of soil, above the permafrost, that thaws in the summer although it refreezes in winter. This is the layer where plants can grow and microorganisms live.

**alpine tundra**   an ecological community of low-growing-plants found at high altitudes; this community has many plant species in common with the Arctic tundra but is found south of the Arctic, mostly on high mountains

**annual**   a plant that lasts only one year or season and must start growing from seed the next year or season

**biome**   an area that has a certain kind of climate and a certain kind of community of plants and animals

**circumpolar**   around the earth, near one of the Poles

**consumer**   an animal that cannot make its own food, but must eat plants and/or other animals

**ecologist**   a scientist who studies living things and how they interact with one another and their environment

**ecotone**   a border between two biomes, where the plants and animals of those biomes mix

**food chain**   a simplified diagram showing the transfer of energy from the sun to a plant, from that plant to a plant eater, and from the plant eater to a meat eater, and so on

**food web**   a diagram that shows energy flow in a community by showing how the food chains in that community are linked

**global warming**   the predicted change in the earth's climate caused by the buildup of pollutants in the earth's atmosphere. The end results may be rising sea levels, and shifting weather patterns, *not* an overall global warming as once thought.

**hibernation**   an animal's sluggish state of reduced metabolism and reduced body temperature that helps it survive winter

**isotherm**   an imaginary line that bounds an area where certain temperatures occur

**mutualistic**   a relationship that benefits all parties involved

**perennial**   a plant that does not die in winter, but instead regrows each year, from underground roots

**permafrost**   frozen ground

**plant biomass**   the weight of all the plant matter—roots, shoots, stems, and other plant parts—for a given area

**polar desert**   a biome north of the tundra, where very few plants grow

**producer**   an organism, such as a plant, that can make its own food

**solifluction**   the slow creep downhill of soggy soil. This is caused by gravity

**species diversity**   the number of different kinds of plants and animals in a given area

**taiga**   a biome that is characterized by conifers such as spruce, fir, and tamarack, and occurs north of the temperate deciduous forest

**tussocks**   mounds formed by plants such as cotton grass

# INDEX